21 世纪有影响力画家个案研究

易 凯 YI KAI

21SHIJI YOU YINGXIANGLI HUAJIA GEAN
YANJIU

目 录

二十一世纪有影响力画家易凯个案研究

主编感言

易凯先生是一位既勤于实践，又善于思考的旅美艺术家，曾就读于北京解放军艺术学院国画专业，又就读于中央民族大学油画研究生班，绘画基本功扎实，深谙东西方绘画的理念与画法，练就了全面的艺术技能。自1990年赴美之后，又受西方现代主义的影响，涌动着寻求新的艺术话语的强烈冲动，开始转向更能凸现他内心深处由中西文化撞击所产生的困惑和探索——抽象画的研究，并在国际画坛上取得令人瞩目的成就。

他是根据几个方面的因素来决定自己艺术道路的：对绘画本质的思索，对当前世界绘画大格局的审视，从自己的素养和能力出发。他希望把自己的感觉、感情、观念，诉诸于绘画的过程，诉诸于形和色彩以及绘画语言无穷尽的变化中。由此，他尝试了各种艺术表现手法，使用过多种媒介、材质，终于依靠着坚定的艺术信念和必有所成的决心，找到了一种用点、线、面、色彩、形体、构图等元素重新构造他心灵独特感觉的艺术形式。

易凯的着眼点是用西方现代艺术的技法、手段改造中国绘画，也就是用西方绘画的表现方法、技巧和西方的现代艺术观念画出富有中国文化精神的作品。在他的作品中，饱含着中国传统文化的底蕴，结合西方绘画之真谛，创作出风格独特的、自由抒情的抽象绘画，引领我们走进了一个超越客观实体的意象世界。易凯抽象主义绘画并非是他脱离现实主义的主观臆造，当他在画面上挥动调和颜色的画笔时，他的直接和间接的生活经验，都会融化为他的创作灵感和资源。艺术实践表明，易凯是一位十分重视体悟生活和艺术奥秘的艺术家。

本画册所发表的作品和照片，就是易凯和他的美国朋友——佩吉和戴夫夫妇赴中国西部地区饱游饫看后的生活记录和印象。从拉萨到敦煌，从吐鲁番到喀什，行程逾万里，历时二十余天，美国朋友用的是摄影镜头，易凯用的是绘画形式，艺术地再现了雪域高原与丝绸之路的风土人情、人文景观。易凯凭藉他坚实的造型能力和全面的艺术技能，对所见的人物、建筑进行了写实主义的表现，主要以钢笔速写为主，或以淡墨渲染，或施以素描层次，或以彩墨泼洒，创造了纸上的生命。无论是人物的肖像、动态，还是古老建筑的整体、局部，抑或是大场面的宏观处理，都线条流畅，层次清晰，形象质朴，生动感人，没有矫情和造作，具有鲜明的艺术个性。在这些作品中，易凯将中国画以线造型的功力与西画的明暗造型巧妙地结合在一起，显示的是东方的、中国的情韵，吐露的是自己真实的感情，追求的是一种心灵与自然交融的境界。

艺术档案

■ 易 凯

■ 1955年出生于湖南省长沙市。1971年入伍，1983年毕业于北京解放军艺术学院美术系国画专业，获文学学士学位，1988年毕业于中央民族大学美术系油画研究生班，获文学硕士学位。1982年加入中国美术家协会。1990年赴美国，现设艺术工作室于美国洛杉矶。

■ 1975年以后，作品曾多次参加全国美展。1988年在北京中国美术馆举办三人联展，1989年后在日本、新加坡、美国及中国台湾、香港等地多次举办个人画展。

■ 作品收藏于美国明尼阿波利斯艺术博物馆、明尼苏达州美国艺术博物馆、香港艺倡画廊及其他博物馆和艺术机构。

■ 作品曾获1981年中国青年美展铜奖、1985年北京市美展最佳作品奖。1996年获美国明尼苏达州艺术博物馆馆长选择奖，2000年作品受美国国家艺术博物馆长提名。

卢可斯的几句话

佩吉和戴维在高昌古城
Peggy & Dave in XinJiang

戴夫·卢卡斯是一位退休的放射科医生，他对摄影却始终情有独钟。1965年，在离结束伊朗和平队任务还有二年时，他便买下了有生以来的第一部高档照相机。

戴夫多次参加专业摄影学习班，还曾出席在 Santa Fe 和摩洛哥举办的旅游摄影家学会年会。

戴夫热衷于山水和自然风光的摄影。也许是长期从事放射线学研究工作的缘故，戴夫对构图和光影有着特殊的敏感和迷恋。摩洛哥的沙丘、戈壁沙漠、美国蒙大纳州和爱达荷州滚动的麦浪，都是他摄影作品的题材。苏比列湖冬天冰封的过程，也成为他作品的主题。

佩吉·卢卡斯拥有社会工作学科的硕士学位，却并没有从事与其专业相关的职业，而是成为了一个房屋开发公司的成功合伙人。佩吉一直对摄影怀有极大的兴趣，她没有接受有关摄影的专业培训，但伴随戴夫参加专业摄影学习班使她对摄影更加入迷。

佩吉的爱好是拍摄人物，特别是孩子的照片。她经常带着相机去超市、运动场和公园，捕捉和拍摄人们真实生活的瞬间。佩吉出生在中国西南省份，她的父亲是中国人。也许是因为出生地和那遥远的记忆缘故，佩吉被中国少数民族文化深深地吸引而流连忘返。

佩吉和戴夫的婚后生活里，包括了大量的时光在世界各地旅行。他们曾作为和平队成员志愿到伊朗的南部工作，在那里，他们迷恋上了游牧民族 Gashgai。随后，他们又接受公共健康服务机构的委派，前往纳瓦霍人部落工作了两年。在美国明尼阿波利斯市定居，之后有了二个儿子。在这段美好的时光里，他们时常全家外出度假，美国蒙大纳州、尤卡坦半岛、佛罗里达洲西海岸和西欧国家成为了他们全家人的度假圣地。他们拍摄了大量的旅游风光照片，两个儿子也拿起了相机加入了家庭的拍摄队伍，结果证明两个儿子都有摄影天赋。

孩子们上大学后，戴夫将在医院工作的时间减少，使他有了更多的时间去专研摄影。他和佩吉至少每年出国旅游两次，他们总是被具有本土传统文化的国家所吸引。他们曾去过新西兰、秘鲁、土耳其、坦桑尼亚和印度等国家。他们三次来中国旅游，佩吉还沿着当年父母在日本侵略中国时的逃难路线探寻他们当年的足迹。他们被中国西南、西藏和丝绸之路的自然风光和独特的本土文化久久陶醉。

摄影成为了他们旅游生活中的重要组成部分，旅游中的"亮点"时时向他们挑战，旅行箱里各种镜头和三脚架，成打的胶卷伴随着他们的旅游生活。1999年，他们开始改用数码相机。从此，他们的摄影生活又开始了新的篇章。

回顾他们的摄影作品，显而易见，各地土族居民的生活习俗和艺术成为他们的作品亮点。在这四十多年的摄影生涯里，他们拍摄了大量的有关 Gashgai，美国纳瓦霍人、霍皮人、肯尼亚和坦桑尼亚的马赛人、北非的柏柏尔人的文化传统照片。他们拍摄的西藏风光和丝绸之路的照片，体现了他们作品的风格，与艺术家易凯同道旅行的机会，使他们的旅游摄影作品更增添了艺术的色彩。

（翻译：董凯）

姐妹仨　46cm × 58cm　钢笔纸本
Three sisters　15" × 19"　Ink on paper

Words from Dave & Peggy

Dave Lucas is a retired radiologist. He has always had an interest in photography and bought his first "good" camera in 1965 just before he left for two years of Peace Corps duty in Iran.

Dave has participated in numerous photography workshops including travel photography sessions in Santa Fe and Morocco.

Dave is drawn to landscape and nature photography. Perhaps because of his career in radiology he is fascinated by subtle shadows and forms .The sand dunes of Morocco and the Gobi desert are favorite subjects as are the rolling wheat fields of Montana and Idaho. He is fascinated by the winter ice formations of Lake Superior.

Peggy Lucas has a master degree in social work but spent her career as a partner in a housing development company. She has always loved to take pictures but has never really studied photography although she accompanied Dave on travel workshops and found them fascinating.
Peggy loves to take pictures of people, especially children. She is drawn to markets, playgrounds and parks so that she can capture images of people in real life settings.

Peggy's father was Chinese and she was born in Southwest China where many tribal cultures flourish. Perhaps it is that long ago memory that has attracted her to the unique ethnic cultures.

Peggy and Dave's married life has included extensive world travel. They spent two years in the Peace Corps where they served in southern Iran. While there they became fascinated by the migrating Gashgai tribes. This was followed by a two year assignment in the Public Health Service where they lived on the Navajo reservation.

Dave and Peggy settled in Minneapolis where they raised two sons. During this time there were countless family vacations. Montana, the Yucatan, Florida's west coast and Western Europe were common destinations and they became photo excursions as well. Both boys were given good cameras and both proved to have excellent photographic instincts.

After the boys went to college Dave cut back on his Radiology practice so that he could spend more time with his photography. He and Peggy tried to take at least two significant foreign trips a year and again they were attracted to places with interesting indigenous cultures... New Zealand, Peru, Turkcy, Tanzania and India.. They also made three trips to China where Peggy retraced her parents travels as refugees from the Japanese invasion. They were particularly attracted to Southwest China, Tibet and the Silk Road.

Photography has always been an important part of their travel. Traveling "light" was always challenging since luggage always included tripods and a variety of lenses. Many of these trips included dozens of rolls of film but in 1999 they both converted to digital cameras and their whole photo experience was transformed!

In looking backward at their photographic work it is clear that indigenous people and their customs and art have become focal points. The Gashgai, the Navajo, the Hopi, The Masai, the Berber, and countless other cultures have been photographed by them in a period of over 40 years. The photos of Tibet and the Silk Road are typical of these studies but in this case they were privileged to travel with Yi Kai who added an added artistic dimension to their travel photos.

哥俩　28cm × 37cm　钢笔纸本　Brother 9" × 12" Ink on paper

出版前的几句话　　■ 易　凯／文

我与卢可斯夫妇相识于上世纪 90 年代中期。他们两次随我来华旅游，朝夕相处的时光使我们由相识而成为朋友。

2004 年秋天，我们一行 20 人由上海入关，经成都赴拉萨然后转道兰州、嘉裕关、敦煌、吐鲁番、乌鲁木齐，最后抵达丝绸之路的重镇喀什，行程逾万里，为期二十余天。

此次旅行属观光性质，在每一个城市停留时间不长。除我之外，其他 20 人都未到过这些地方。20 余天的游历于我是旧地重游，对他们却是从未有过的视觉和生活体验。

作为有中美两地生活经历的我，重游旧地更多是以一种审视的眼光在观察 20 余年来的变化，比较现在和过去的差别。作为一批外来文化的旅游者，他们对所见所闻却是兴奋、激动地照单全收。

20 余天的游历，积累了上千幅的照片，我们视其为人生经历的记载，

也是这次游历的印象。将这些记载和印象用摄影和速写的形式体现出来并结集出版，是旅行结束时我们三人定下来要完成的一件事。

三年过去了，我们三人从繁杂的日常生活中挤出时间完成了这本集子。翻阅印刷小样总感觉还有不少有待改进和增删的地方。好在我们三人计划出几本视觉游记，因此有些遗憾尚可在将来去补偿。而此书的出版也算成全了我们将这次旅游经历与大家分享的一个期望。

I first met Dr. and Mrs. Lucas in the middle of the 1990s, and became very good friends after spending two tours through China together.

During our 20 people trip in the fall of 2004, the Lucases and I entered China from Shanghai, then proceeded to Chengdu City, then Lhasa, Lanzhou, Jiayuguan, Dunhuang, Tulufan, Urumqi, and then finally arriving in Kashi. This was a famed town on the Silk Road known for its history and culture. We traveled for a period of 20 days, and many thousands of miles.

Since it was primarily a sightseeing tour, we spent only brief periods in each city. As opposed to me, this was the first time passing through these places for many of the travelers. This gave me a renewed sense of visual perception, as well as a vague sentiment of familiarity.

While traversing through these nostalgic landmarks, it was hard not to notice some of the changes that had occurred in the past 20 years. This is partly due to the recent economical, cultural and political advancements of China, but also conributing to these perceived changes were my enriched life experiences. Living in the United States for over 15 years, the necessary survival instincts of assimilation and amalgamation has instilled in me a dual-perspective. It is as if my personal empiricism draws from two realms of concepts, then constructing notions and ideas with two sets of blueprints. It was hard to ignore this dichotomous aspect of my being.

We captured the highlights of our 20 day tour in thousands of photos. It was not until after the trip that the Lucases and I decided to work through our experiences and reproduce them in the media of photos, paintings, and pen sketches.

This collection has taken three years to complete. It is to our regret that even reading through this final draft that we have found many areas that should have been added, deleted or consummated. Fortunately we plan to work out several more visual tour collections in the future to compensate. We see that this is more fitting since this is not meant to be a perfect capture of our experiences or of the places. It is an attempt to reconstruct a particular moment in time, and

数钱的喇嘛　38cm × 33cm　钢笔纸本　Need donation 10" × 13" Ink on paper

encourage a particular recollection of experience. As a Chinese proverb states, "the palest ink lasts longer than the most retentive memory", we treat this work as a time capsule of those 20 days.

Words for this book

Betty Ritter

Yi Kai and the Lucases started this book in 2004. Global Harmony Through Art joins their creatively in support of this project. Yi Kai is Executive Director of the above organization. We are happy that it is now ready for publication.

Global Harmony Through Art was founded by Yi Kai and Betty Ritter in 2004. It was in an effort to encourage peace and harmony in the world. We were concerned that our country went to war with a county that was not at war with them. Our idea was that artists could work together using their non-verbal language to communicate and establish friendships accross cultures.

I,Betty Ritter,have known Yi Kai for many years and appreciate his depth and beauty of art expression. He has a profound gift for conceiving ideas and capturing them with the Lucases photos ,which you will be able to enjoy in these pages.

美国艺术促进世界和平基金会非常高兴地看到由基金会从2004年开始一直关注和支持的一个艺术项目,在基金会艺术总监易凯策划和参与创作的《印象》一书终于出版发行了。

美国艺术促进世界和平基金会由易凯和我——帕奇·悦塔创立于2004年,我们的宗旨是努力促进世界各国的和平和融洽相处。我们认识到即使国家与另一个国家处于战争状态也不代表一个国家和另一个国家的人民交战。我们的想法是艺术家们可以在一起合作,使用其独特的艺术语言进行交流,并增进不同文化背景下人类的相互理解和友谊。

我认识易凯已有多年,本人非常欣赏他对艺术的深刻理解以及其独特的艺术创作。大家可以通过本书的画面来欣赏他的艺术作品。

美国艺术 促进世界和平基金会主席 Betty Ritter,
易凯及夫人郑俭 2006 年于上海

布达拉宫远眺　Portola Palace

布达拉宫的门、窗　Portola Palace door & window

寺庙的窗户　Window of Temple

布达拉宫　34cm × 62cm　钢笔、丙烯纸本
Portola Palace　11" × 22"　Ink & Acrylic on paper

From the collection of Pat & Vincent Schaefer

阳光下的寺庙之窗　40cm × 27cm　钢笔、水墨纸本
Window under sunshine　13" × 9"　Ink on paper

From the collection of David Yi

多年的转经筒　46cm × 60cm　钢笔、水墨纸本
Greasy prayer wheels　15" × 20"　Ink on paper

寺庙画工的颜料盘　Paint bowls

庙门　Door

多年的转经筒　Greasy prayer wheels

寺庙的门、窗　36cm × 54cm　钢笔、丙烯纸本
Door & Window of Temple　12" × 18"　Ink & Acrylic on paper

庙门　39cm × 38cm　钢笔、丙烯纸本
Door of Temple　13" × 13"　Ink & Acrylic on paper

From the collection of Dolly Fiterman

寺庙　38cm × 36cm　钢笔、水墨纸本
Temple　13" × 12"　Ink on paper

寺庙的结构一　38cm × 51cm　钢笔、水墨纸本
Structure of Temple # 1　13" × 17"　Ink on paper

寺庙的结构二　42cm × 54cm　彩墨纸本
Structure of Temple #2　14" × 18"　Acrylic & Ink on paper

舞动的经幡　22cm × 66cm　钢笔、丙烯纸本
Danceing of prayer flag 7" × 22" Ink & Acrylic on paper

蓝天里的经幡　Prayer flag pole

From the collection of Jian Zheng

经幡的印象　36cm × 56cm　钢笔、丙烯纸本
Impression of prayer flag　12" × 19"　Ink & Acrylic on paper

From the collection of Dave & Peggy Lucas

佛山　Scarves Hillside Buddha

寺顶的壁饰　Freshly Painted

甘丹寺　Ganden Monestary

转经筒　Prayer wheels

寺庙里的经堂　Monk robe

喇嘛　36cm × 46cm　钢笔纸本
Monks　14" × 18"　Ink on paper

三个喇嘛　40cm × 44cm　钢笔、丙烯纸本
Three Monks　13" × 15"　Ink & Acrylic on paper

三个喇嘛　Three Monks

阳光下的寺庙　Temple under sunshine

喇嘛　35cm × 23cm　钢笔、水墨纸本
Monk　12" × 7"　Ink on paper

寺庙中的喇嘛 Monk on stairs

打水的喇嘛 Monk get water

找水的喇嘛　37cm × 27cm　钢笔纸本
Monk got water　12" × 9"　Ink on paper

牦牛和经幡 Yak & prayer flags

找水的喇嘛 Monk got water

负重的牦牛 Yak carries blankets

阳光下　33cm × 31cm　钢笔、丙烯纸本
Sunshine　11" × 10"　Ink & Acrylic on paper

From the collection of Dave & Peggy Lucas

女香客　Woman in Temple

阳光下的香客　Pilgrim under sunshine

吹鼓手　28cm × 34cm　钢笔纸本
Eulogist 11" × 14" Ink on paper

藏妇　30cm × 27cm　钢笔纸本
Tibet lady 12" × 11" Ink on paper

经幡　Prayer flags

大昭寺前的广场　Da Zhao Square

老香客之一　Old pilgrim [#] 1

老香客之二　Old pilgrim [#] 2

老香客之三　55cm × 46cm　钢笔纸本
Old pilgrim # 3　18" × 12"　Ink on paper

From the collection of Dolly Fiterman

阳光下的香客　Fur-lined Pilgrim　　　　　　　穿黄衣的香客　Yellow shirt pilgrim

香客　46cm × 34cm　钢笔、水墨纸本
Pilgrim　15" × 11"　Ink on paper

数佛珠的香客　54cm × 40cm　钢笔、水墨纸本
Pilgrim　18" × 13"　Ink on paper

大昭寺前的香客　Pilgrims

大昭寺前　Da Zhao Square

大昭寺内　Inside of Da Zhao Temple

还俗的喇嘛　58cm × 41cm　钢笔、水墨纸本
Monk　17" × 12"　Ink on paper

From the collection of Pat & Jim Suchan

长发香客　54cm × 40cm　钢笔纸本
Long hari pilgrim　18" × 13"　Ink on paper

八角街头的老太太　33cm × 25cm　钢笔纸本
Old lady in Barkhor Square　11" × 8"　Ink on paper

老太太　Old woman flat

饱经风霜的头像　Frizzy face

高原上的居民　43cm × 45cm　钢笔、水墨纸本
Old man of the highland　14" × 15"　Ink on paper

进香的女人们　60cm × 46cm　钢笔纸本
Tibet ladys　20" × 15"　Ink on paper

女人和喇嘛 45cm × 46cm 钢笔、水墨纸本
Monk with woman 15" × 15" Ink on paper

母与女　38cm × 28cm　钢笔、水墨纸本
Mother with daughter　13" × 9"　Ink on paper

From the collection of Patty Connelly

母与子　42cm × 30cm　钢笔纸本
Mother with Son　14" × 10"　Ink on paper

From the collection of Patty Connelly

母与子　46cm × 47cm　钢笔纸本
Mother with Son　15" × 16"　Ink on paper

大昭寺的清晨 Morning of Da Zhao Temple

正午的八角街 Noon of Barkhor Square

少女　37cm × 28cm　钢笔纸本
Girl　12" × 9"　Ink on paper

香客　38cm × 28cm　钢笔纸本
Pilgrim　13" × 9"　Ink on paper

老人　37cm × 28cm　钢笔纸本
Old lady　12" × 9"　Ink on paper

汉子　38cm × 28cm　钢笔纸本
Tibet man　13" × 9"　Ink on paper

藏女　Tibet women

藏女的头饰　29cm × 38cm　钢笔纸本
Hair decoration　9" × 13"　Ink on paper

藏女的头饰和胸饰　Tibet women's hair & necklace

藏女　Tibet women

数珠的香客　37cm × 28cm　钢笔纸本
Pilgrim　12" × 9"　Ink on paper

微笑的女人　37cm × 28cm　钢笔纸本
Woman　12" × 9"　Ink on paper

戴帽的男人　33cm × 28cm　钢笔纸本
Old man　11" × 9"　Ink on paper

恬静的母子　36cm × 28cm　钢笔纸本
Mother & baby　12" × 9"　Ink on paper

From the collection of Erkang Zheng

丝路印象　34cm × 46cm　钢笔、水墨、丙烯纸本
Impression of silkroad　11" × 15"　Ink & Acrylic on paper

坟地　Graveyard

骆驼　Camel

离开高原　Leaving Tibet

高昌古城　34cm × 60cm　钢笔、丙烯、水墨纸本
Old town of Gaochang 15" × 20"　Ink & Acrylic on paper

From the collection of Ken & Denise Johnson

喀什小巷　46cm × 31cm　钢笔、水墨纸本
Alley of Kashi　15" × 10"　Ink on paper

赶集　28cm × 37cm　钢笔纸本
Go to the local market　9" × 12"　Ink on paper

三代人　31cm × 46cm　钢笔纸本
Three generation　10" × 15"　Ink on paper

老人　37cm × 28cm　钢笔纸本
Old man　12" × 9"　Ink on paper

中年汉子　37cm × 28cm　钢笔纸本
Man　12" × 9"　Ink on paper

From the collection of Pat & Jim Suchan

塔吉克少女　37cm × 28cm　钢笔纸本
Tajike girls　12" × 9"　Ink on paper

三个哥们　28cm × 37cm　钢笔纸本
Three brothers　9" × 12"　Ink on paper

黑衣妇人　Old woman in black

好老头　Nice grey beard

夫妇　38cm × 29cm　钢笔、水墨纸本
Husband & wife　13" × 10"　Ink on paper

From the collection of Lynn Vanlandingham

做馕人　Nan baker

馕　Nan

馕饼店　42cm × 35cm　钢笔、水墨纸本
Nan baker　14" × 12"　Ink on paper

摆摊的老人　46cm × 32cm　钢笔、水墨纸本
Market man　15" × 10"　Ink on paper

摆摊的老人 Market man

聊天 Bearded men

三步曲　Three step

三步曲　46cm × 58cm　钢笔、水墨纸本
Three Step　15" × 19"　Ink on paper

西藏印象
IMPRESSION OF TIBET